THE
FUNNIEST
WEST HAM
QUOTES...
EVER!

Also available to buy

THE FUNNIEST WEST HAM QUOTES.... EVER!

by Gordon Law

gordonlawauthor@yahoo.com

Printed in the United States of America
ISBN-13: 978-1548694494
ISBN-10: 1548694495

Photos courtesy of: CosminIftode/Shutterstock.com; Mitch Gunn/Shutterstock.com

Contents

Introduction

When it comes to real football personalities, there are few more engaging than Harry Redknapp.

The affable cockney was a loyal servant to West Ham United as a player and manager and supplied the media with many hilarious quotes. Redknapp's ability to see the funny side of things, while also having a penchant to lose his temper, makes him hugely entertaining.

Like Redknapp, Paolo Di Canio was another colourful Hammer who shot from the hip with controversial statements.

Even the West Ham boardroom has provided laughs, with Karren Brady firing off broadsides and David Gold triggering social media storms with his bonkers tweets.

On the terraces, West Ham supporters are among the wittiest in the country and their chant about ex-defender Rio Ferdinand was voted the funniest of the last decade.

There's been comic one-liners from Julian Dicks and Frank McAvennie, while recent stars Rob Green and Andy Carroll are among the players who have shown their humorous side. The likes of former managers Alan Curbishley, Glenn Roeder and Sam Allardyce have come out with some great gaffes and bloopers.

Many of their craziest comments can be found in this unique collection of Hammers rib-ticklers and I hope you laugh as much reading this book as I did in compiling it.

Gordon Law

THE FUNNIEST WEST HAM QUOTES... EVER!

CAN YOU MANAGE?

"When you are buying a dog, there are always 10 reasons not to. Because you can't go out more, if you are travelling it's a problem, he's going to pee here and there until he learns, he's going to bite your cat, he's going to leave your place smelly."

Slaven Bilic responds to the idea that you should never return to a former club

"I enjoy big games and I usually win them."

Alan Pardew – before the 2006 FA Cup final defeat

"Bad results slaughter me, they gut me."

Harry Redknapp

Can You Manage?

Reporter: "Harry, what message did you give the players at half-time?"

Harry Redknapp: "Just 'play the same as we did first half'. What do you fucking think I said to them at half-time?"

Reporter: "Dunno."

Harry Redknapp: "'Go and f*cking sit back and let them attack us' or summink? Is that what you think I said? What a fucking stupid question."

"All this tippy tappy stuff everybody keeps going on about as the right way to play football is all a load of b*llocks."

Sam Allardyce

"We have to score more goals than we concede to win a game of football."

Sam Allardyce gets to grips with the rules

"I admit, to the man in the street I might appear very arrogant. There is an arrogance about me and I have to keep an eye on it."

Alan Pardew

"I've learned my lesson with the foreigners. I won't be buying any more of them in the near future."

Harry Redknapp, shortly before signing Titi Camara and Rigobert Song in 2000

"They can make anyone look good. I signed Marco Boogers off a video. He was a good player but a nutter. They didn't show that on the video."

Harry Redknapp on signing players from video tapes

"I don't like people who drain my time and energy. If you've seen the Harry Potter films, we use the term 'dementors' – people who can draw the life out of you in terms of your energy. So we eradicate the 'dementors', encourage the positive people, and that spreads around to create the team spirit we have here."

Alan Pardew

"You need players with big balls at West Ham. The one thing I ask of a player before signing is, 'Can you handle the 35,000 crowds? Because you'll get stick'. 'Oi mate, you're fat, you've got big ears, a fat arse, a big hooter. You're ugly. I'll do your bird a favour if I see her down the pub'."

Alan Pardew

"I tape over most of them with Corrie or Neighbours. Most of them are crap. They can f*cking make anyone look good. I signed Marco Boogers off a video. He was a good player but a nutter. They didn't show that on the video."

Harry Redknapp on the danger of signing players from video tapes

Can You Manage?

"I threw a plate of sandwiches at Don Hutchison. He sat there, still arguing with me, with cheese and tomato running down his face. You can't do that anymore, especially with all the foreigners. They'd go home."

Harry Redknapp

"All that 'happy losers' stuff is a load of cobblers. I hate losing."

Billy Bonds

"As a manager, you accept that you need a double skin – a rhino's and an elephant's – just to survive in the job."

Sam Allardyce

"The managers who've been around a long time don't wear headpieces, they don't have three-way communication with people all round the stadium, they're football managers and they manage."

Alan Curbishley

"I won't ever be going to a top-four club because I'm not called Allardici, just Allardyce."

Sam Allardyce

"I don't know the Spanish for 'On me head, son' but I'm working on it."

Alan Pardew on communicating with Carlos Tevez and Javier Mascherano

"Yeah, yeah. Of course I like it when we are winning. Of course it is brilliant! It is like when you come to a pub that is full of women! You will like it!"

Slaven Bilic

"My idea of sports science was to tackle the wall in the gym, nut the door and throw a few 'f*cks' about before going out to play! That's the only sports science I knew."

Billy Bonds

"I've got coaching badges but they came out of a Corn Flakes packet."

Harry Redknapp

"To me, there's no point in having confrontation for the sake of it. Look at Ruud Gullit. Can you tell me that he was a shrewd manager in what he did to Rob Lee, who was captain of Newcastle and Alan Shearer's best mate? Why make problems for yourself?"

Harry Redknapp on Ruud Gullit's treatment of Rob Lee and Alan Shearer at Newcastle

"You can't be like a small child and cry and go, 'Buy me that Kinder Egg' that my daughter is asking me for every time we go to Waitrose. Then if you don't buy it she is very disappointed. You can't be like that. You move on."

Slaven Bilic is frustrated West Ham couldn't sign Sporting Lisbon's William Carvalho

Can You Manage?

"When I speak to top coaches about a player, they will say, 'He's quick. He's fast'. In the Croatian Second Division, the manager will tell me, 'His anaerobic endurance is 1.2 cross metres squared in a second'. And then people on the next table, the chairmen, say 'Oh, f*cking hell, he's clever'."

Slaven Bilic

"I was in bed with my wife last night – if you're as ugly as me you want to talk about football. And she said, 'Harry, if you're drawing, push Trevor Sinclair up front'. So I gambled and it worked."

Harry Redknapp

THE FUNNIEST WEST HAM QUOTES... EVER!

BOARDROOM BANTER

"I told my chairman that David O'Leary paid £18m for Rio Ferdinand and Leeds have given him £5m in share options. I bring in £18m and all I get is a bacon sandwich."

Harry Redknapp

"You're not alone, lots of people like Donald Trump. Millions of people liked Adolf Hitler and lived to regret it."

David Gold's tweet compares the US presidential candidate Donald Trump to Adolf Hitler

"This comes from a man who also endorses Viagra, at least that's one product that stands up!"

Karren Brady takes a swipe at Pele and his commercial endorsements

"I really want to whack Birmingham. I have a great fondness for them but it was sad the way it ended. They reneged on the decision to keep me on the board. That will always rankle."

David Gold on his former club

"It's like us calling it the Ann Summers stadium."

David Sullivan on Manchester City's stadium sponsorship deal with Etihad

"Rather than the super scorer we hoped for, we acquired a super-size, a player devoted to filling his belly more than filling the net."

Karren Brady on Benni McCarthy

"I saw so many things in my life and in football for me, it was nothing. Woman and football, it's not such a good combination."

Benni McCarthy hits back at Karren Brady

"More importantly Benni, footballers and beef burgers don't mix."

David Gold makes a fat joke at Benni McCarthy after the striker criticised Karren Brady

"It makes me want to throw up. There's the devil with a set of t*ts."

Benni McCarthy has a pop at Karren Brady

"Nice of him. But Benni, I'm meant to have t*ts, you aren't!"

Karren Brady's witty response to Benni McCarthy's dig

"Benni McCarthy was a big fat mistake. It could be worse as across the river Fernando Torres, at £50million, remains as thin as two yards of pump water and has not scored either."

Karren Brady

"Perhaps Richard thought I was too busy making the tea and washing up to take his call."

Karren Brady aims fire at Richard Keys after the Sky Sports presenter was caught up in a sexism row

@StuAus: "DG, my goldfish just died, can I have a RT lol"

@davidgold: "NO. You cant have a RT for such a ridiculous reason. PS are you sure it's dead."

David Gold tweets a fan

"All this business, 'I love West Ham'. Well it's 'I love West Ham if they give me £250,000 a week'."

David Sullivan blasts Carlos Tevez's wage demands after talks over a return to the club

"I'm only 27 but I look 60. This club has made my hair turn grey."

David Gold on the stresses of being West Ham chief

"It's funny! It made me laugh."

Slaven Bilic chuckles after Sporting Lisbon's president described the West Ham owners as the "dildo brothers"

"Many times since we took over the club, Paolo Di Canio has approached David Sullivan and David Gold about being the manager of West Ham. I think they considered him briefly – something I never did – but dismissed him on the basis that football and fascism do not mix."

Karren Brady

"I had a tweet from someone who said, 'It's not your club, it's the fans' club'. I tweeted back, 'You're absolutely right. The club belongs to the fans. Only the debts belong to me'."

David Gold

"If Terry Brown said something at a board meeting that I didn't think much of, I'd tell him to his face: 'What a load of b*llocks, you don't know what you're talking about'."

Harry Redknapp

@officialbowers: "I enjoyed your book David but have one question, why?"

@davidgold: "Why, what. I don't understand why you ask me 'why'."

David Gold

"We didn't buy him from Argos."

David Gold wishes he had a 30-day money back guarantee for Andy Carroll

"I thought he treated the ball like a bar of soap –
he couldn't hang onto it! But we're very
happy [to have him back]."
**David Gold on Andy Carroll's return from
injury**

"Alan Sugar isn't always right you know. Anyone
had an Amstrad computer?"
David Sullivan

"One day I realised my father was stealing my
shares. Then I saw my wife having sex with my
best friend."
David Gold

"Winston Wiremu Reid is 28 today. Happy Birthday Winston, have a great season."

David Gold tweets Winston Reid a birthday message – but accompanies it with a photo of Kyle Knoyle

"I am an accountant and I'm very suspicious of everyone in football."

Terry Brown

"If I say to you now there is a 51 per cent or 32.5 per cent chance, it doesn't matter."

Avram Grant responds to David Sullivan's claims that West Ham are 75 per cent likely to be relegated

THE FUNNIEST WEST HAM QUOTES... EVER!

MANAGING PLAYERS

"My missus fancies him. Even I don't know whether to play him or f*ck him."

Harry Redknapp on Dani

"Everybody deserves a second chance – and to be fair, he seems a lot calmer than Tomas Repka!"

Alan Pardew after signing Moses Ashikodi

"He's cocky and arrogant but show him a goal and he's away, like a wind-up toy."

Harry Redknapp on Jermain Defoe

"Have I got anything bad to say about him?
Well he got cautioned by the referee at Burnley
once."

John Lyall on Trevor Brooking

"Samassi Abou don't speak the English too
good."

Harry Redknapp

"Robert Green has bought a lottery ticket and
we asked him for his numbers!"

**Alan Curbishley after keeper Robert
Green's hot streak in a 1-0 win over Arsenal**

"He came to me and said, 'Futre 10'. I said, 'Eusebio, Pele, Maradona 10 – no, f*cking 16'. We argued. He threw the shirt down, trod on it and left."

Harry Redknapp on Paulo Futre

"It's almost like he has Dr Who's TARDIS because he always turns up on time."

Alan Pardew on Teddy Sheringham

"[Samassi] Abou retaliated but the fellow went down as if he was dead, and then started rolling around."

Harry Redknapp

"I used to make sure I put him on a team in training where nobody would kick him, because otherwise it would all blow up. He was volatile. He'd kick one wide and I'd used to say it was a goal. It's Paolo. Got to keep him sweet for Saturday."

Harry Redknapp on Paolo Di Canio's ego

"Hopefully Andy [Carroll] has only tweeted his hamstring."

Sam Allardyce

"John Hartson's got more previous than Jack the Ripper."

Harry Redknapp on John Hartson

"He's a smashing professional and a leader. He's like Bobby Moore in that respect, though he wouldn't have made it into Bobby's drinking school."

Harry Redknapp on Paolo Di Canio

"Tom could pick a fly off Vic's eyebrows."

Manager Charlie Paynter lauds winger Thomas Yews' pin-point crossing for striker Vic Watson

"Joe Cole missed an open goal that my f*cking missus could have scored."

Harry Redknapp

"From a still picture how does anybody know what Di Canio was doing? He might have been signalling to a teammate about a tactic from a corner. He might have been gesturing a tactical change. He could have been showing that the score was 1-0."

Harry Redknapp on Paolo Di Canio's one-fingered gesture to Aston Villa fans

"I don't think it was simulation, I think he just fell over."

Gianfranco Zola defends David Di Michele's 'dive' against Liverpool

LIFESTYLE CHOICE

"I met [England assistant manager] John Gorman during an end-of-season tour in Spain. We were all drinking in a bar and John and I bumped into each other. We had a chat and he told me I'd never play for England unless I grew my hair. I told him to f*ck off."
Julian Dicks

"I'm going down the apples and pears, into the jam jar, down the frog and toad into the rub-da-dub-dub, and I'm going to have pig's ear."
Gianfranco Zola when asked if had learnt any cockney-rhyming slang

"I don't really like the north. It's always raining, it's really cold and I don't like all those little houses."

Frederic Kanoute

"The cook prepares very good food. I prefer to stay here and eat rather than going to my house. But don't tell my wife."

Gianfranco Zola

"The man who comes to take care of my piranhas tells me he will kill all my fish if I leave West Ham."

Paolo Di Canio

"He made us look really weak. He was in there doing all kinds of exercises and Robbie and I just sat there trying to keep warm."

Jack Collison on the time he and Robbie Keane bumped into Frank Bruno in an ice chamber

Q: "Which TV programme would you most like to appear in?"

A: "Thunderbirds. I'd like to fly in Thunderbird II."

Kevin Keen

"I am going to get drunk tonight."

Gianfranco Zola after West Ham snatch a late point at Everton

"We were all on the coach waiting to go to Stockport and [Florin] Raducioiu was in Harvey Nichols shopping with his missus."

Harry Redknapp

"Once you've had a bull terrier, you never want another dog. I've got six bull terriers, a rottweiler and a bulldog."

Julian Dicks

"My chat-up line used to be, 'I know a lot of Page 3 birds – show me your boobs and I'll see how they compare'."

Frank McAvennie

"Golf's meant to be a gentleman's sport but I tended to lose my rag when I fluffed a shot. I ended up smashing loads of my clubs."

Julian Dicks

"About six weeks ago the wife and I went to Spain on holiday and the cash machines weren't working. I didn't have any money for an ice cream for my children, but luckily Harry was there. He granted me 100 euros for my children to have an ice cream. I sent him back a letter with his 100 euros plus 10 per cent. In no way is that a bung, it was purely the interest I know he charges on loans!"

Alan Pardew on being helped out by Harry Redknapp

"I squeezed into some very tight black pants and nailed the Moonwalk. I've even dressed up as Cheryl Cole."

Sam Allardyce likes a bit of fancy dress

"Yes, I was Jack the Lad, everyone knows that. I loved chasing after girls. The chase was great."

Frank McAvennie

"I expect to be in Las Vegas on that day."

Sam Allardyce isn't confident West Ham will be in the play-off final, which is the same day as Amir Khan's big fight

"People cook up some unbelievable stuff for breakfast here. As for eating baked beans at breakfast time, they can trigger off a violent reaction in anybody not used to them."
Herita Ilunga

"I always thought golf was a poof's game. Now I prefer it to football."
Julian Dicks is opening his mind

"With the foreign players it's more difficult. Most of them don't even bother with the golf, they don't want to go racing. They don't even drink."
Harry Redknapp

Lifestyle Choice

"One thing I do know about the new chairman is he's a biscuit baron! When I heard that I was overjoyed and thought 'Yes! Bourbons all round!' I have got a bit of a superstition about eating biscuits the night before a game. I think it must have started at away games. In the hotels they always have those little packets of biscuits and I started having a couple before a game. I always seemed to do well so I carried it on, it stuck. When I come back from my injury maybe the chairman will be able to sort me out with a supply – he could be the perfect chairman. I won't get a goal bonus, I can get a biscuit bonus."

Dean Ashton loves a biscuit as much as new chairman Eggert Magnusson

A FUNNY OLD GAME

"The worst thing was when people phoned up my girlfriend, who is six months pregnant, and asked her, 'What's it like living with a lunatic?'"
John Hartson after his training-ground attack on Eyal Berkovic

"Even when they had Moore, Hurst and Peters, West Ham's average finish was about 17th. It just shows how useless the other eight of us were."
Harry Redknapp on his days as a player

"My mum would kill me if I wore gloves in a game."
Matt Jarvis is no sissy

"The crowd are shouting, 'England's No.1'. I say No.6, so for the moment I am closer!"

Rob Green jokes about his England snub by having 'England's No.6' stitched on to his gloves

"Bellers [Craig Bellamy] looked at me and said, 'You can have it but you better f*cking score'. I scored and I've always taken them since then."

Mark Noble on taking penalties

"The rules of soccer are quite simple. Basically it's this: if it moves, kick it. If it doesn't move, kick it until it does."

Phil Woosnam

"I spent the last half-hour with the crowd spinning and bits of tongue falling off in my mouth but such is life as a goalkeeper, you are going to get these whacks."

Rob Green after clashing with West Brom's Jonas Olsson

"The only relaxed boss is Big Ron. He had me drinking pink champagne – before the match."

Harry Redknapp on Ron Atkinson

"There are two people in my life that are real heroes. One is Lester Piggott and the other is Ron Greenwood."

John Bond

"I'm the last old-fashioned centre-half. They're all fancy dans now. Too many good-looking bastards like Rio Ferdinand who all go out with pop stars."

Neil Ruddock

"For an away team to get a penalty at Old Trafford, Jaap Stam needs to take a machine gun and riddle you full of bullets."

Paolo Di Canio

"If I could have a pound a shirt, I could get a new car!"

Mark Noble on being the biggest shirt-seller in the club shop in 2007

"I just couldn't train in a Brazil shirt. I wouldn't do it. It was like asking an Englishman to wear a German kit – he'd never do that."

Carlos Tevez on his forfeit for storming off after being subbed against Sheffield Utd

"I was watching the TV when all these Man City players were being introduced. And I must admit, I didn't have a clue who they were. I'd never heard of them before."

Mark Noble

"He's disappeared to Azerbaijan, or somewhere ridiculous in the world."

Harry Redknapp on Tony Adams

"Judging by the shape of his face, he must have headed a lot of goals."

Harry Redknapp on Iain Dowie

"There are sections of the crowd who complain but it's why they come to the ground. These fellas get sh*t off the wife all week and they come to football to let it out."

Kevin Nolan

"It was a peach of an effort which left me with no chance of saving."

David James hails teammate Hayden Mullins' own-goal against West Brom

"Bob's got it all now. The old South Bank named after him at Upton Park, statues outside the ground and at Wembley Stadium. They even use his name to sell West Ham United merchandise these days. When he was alive they didn't want to know him. I saw him get slung out of there for not having a ticket."

Harry Redknapp on Bobby Moore

"If I am really honest, a lot of people who now go to football don't really understand the game."

Mark Noble hits back at his West Ham critics

"Immigration has surrounded the Wembley premises! I knew it was a trap! The only way to get out safely is to wear an England jersey and paint your face w/ the St George's flag!"

Carlton Cole tweets during England's friendly with Ghana

"There are already millions of camera angles showing everything, and referees even have things in their ears now. Pretty soon they'll be going out on to the pitch with a satellite dish stuck up their arses."

Ian Wright

THE FUNNIEST WEST HAM QUOTES... EVER!

CALL THE MANAGER

"It was a terrific game, but I'd rather it had been a load of cr*p and we'd won."

Harry Redknapp after the Hammers were knocked out of the FA Cup to Tottenham

"You can't give Kevin Phillips too many chances before he punishes you. I should have left him at Baldock."

Glenn Roeder had plucked the striker from non-league football while Watford manager

"Even the chef's been out for two weeks with a hernia."

Alan Curbishley

"I'm just glad I don't have to pay it."

Alan Curbishley on West Ham's record £5.5m fine for fielding ineligible players Carlos Tevez and Javier Mascherano

"It was nothing."

Harry Redknapp on the training ground clash which saw John Hartson kick teammate Eyal Berkovic in the head

"What he [John Hartson] did was totally out of order."

Harry Redknapp reconsiders his earlier view after the public's reaction to it

THE FUNNIEST WEST HAM QUOTES... EVER!

"You can't get f*ck-all for a million nowadays."
Harry Redknapp on the £1m he paid for
Hammers flop Marco Boogers

"If you took the goals out of it, I think it was pretty even."
Alan Curbishley on the 4-0 rout by Chelsea

"Let's talk about Andy Carroll, let's talk about Randolph, let's talk about Mark Noble, for f*ck sake!"
Slaven Bilic gets irritated after journalists ask about Dimitri Payet's future

"When training, Oxo is the only beverage used by our team and speak of the supreme strength and power of endurance which they have derived from its use."

Manager Sydney King on the magical powers of the beef drink

"I've just been given a video recording of the game and I'm going to tape Neighbours over it."

Harry Redknapp can't bare to watch West Ham's goalless draw with Southampton

"He can't take it because we've out-tactic-ed him, outwitted him. He just can't cope. He can tell me all he wants. I don't give a sh*te. I love to see Chelsea players moaning at the referee, trying to intimidate him, Jose jumping up and down saying we play crap football. It's brilliant when you get a result against him."

Sam Allardyce on Jose Mourinho's claim that West Ham played "football from the 19th century" to get a 0-0 draw at Chelsea

"It all started with the resilience at Chelsea, you know, the 19th-century defending, which has grown us into the 21st century perhaps."

Sam Allardyce has a dig at Jose Mourinho after West Ham's victory

"As soon as I did it, I realised what I'd done. I'm not the dancer, I'm usually the bloke at the bar."

Alan Pardew on his touchline jig to celebrate the winner in the 2006 FA Cup semi-final success over Middlesbrough

"I was offered him about four years ago when he was only 19. I remember watching him play in a game against Barnet reserves – he looked decent enough but this was just after I had all those problems with the Romanian lads and I thought the last thing I needed was a Ukrainian."

Harry Redknapp on turning down the chance to buy Andriy Shevchenko

"We're in a very exciting cup tie with a massive, massive feeling of joy at the end of it."

Sam Allardyce ahead of West Ham's first leg League Cup semi-final against Man City. The Hammers lost 6-0 and then 3-0

"I've seen better fights at a wedding."

Harry Redknapp on a training ground row between Alvin Martin and Matthew Rush

"I think I still have a couple of his studs in my ankle I can give back to him."

Gianfranco Zola on locking horns with Roy Keane

"Chico Flores was squealing. Centre halves are not supposed to squeal."

Sam Allardyce after referee Howard Webb sent off Andy Carroll for an apparent elbow on the Swansea defender

"I can assure West Ham fans that no stone will be unearthed in our preparation for next week."

Alan Pardew won't be preparing then?

"We were pumping in crosses when we should have been cuddling the ball."

Alan Curbishley looks for a little more finesse

"First of all I had to find the bloody cabinet. When I eventually did, I opened the doors and out flew two bats, three Japanese soldiers and Lord Lucan!"

Harry Redknapp on West Ham's trophy cabinet

"I've brought in a replacement already in Yassin Moutaouakil, who I feel is going to give real competition to Luke whether he stays or not."

Alan Pardew after Middlesbrough offer £2.5m for Luke Young. But if he's gone then there's no competition?

"The lad went home to the Ivory Coast and got a bit of food poisoning. He must have eaten a dodgy missionary or something."

Harry Redknapp on Samassi Abou

"I suppose in the end we couldn't cope with long-ball United."

Sam Allardyce has a dig at Man United's style of play after they got a late equaliser

"We parked the bus but we didn't put the handbrake on. It was simply great defending when we didn't have the ball."

Slaven Bilic after West Ham's 3-0 win over Liverpool

"Where are we in relation to Europe? Not too far from Dover."

Harry Redknapp plays down West Ham's chances of qualifying for Europe

"I'm flattered by the response from fans who believe I should be the next boss, but two and two do not always make four."

Alan Curbishley's maths don't add up

"I was going to pull him off at half-time, but he got a piece of orange like everyone else."

Harry Redknapp on Paolo Di Canio

Journalist: "What's happening about Marco Negri, Harry?"

Harry: "Negri? Don't know what you are talking about? Who's he?"

Journalist: "That bloke from Rangers running around the training ground behind you."

Harry: "Oh that Negri. Yeah we are having a look at him."

Harry gets to grips with foreign trialists

"Everyone f*cking jumps all over you. They don't care Michael Carrick's just 19. When he gave the ball away the other week there was 20,000 people c*nting him off. He give a bad ball and they are all f*cking 'weeerrrr'."

Harry Redknapp on West Ham fans

THE FUNNIEST WEST HAM QUOTES... EVER!

TALKING
BALLS

Aaron Cresswell: "You know, wait till I am back in training and you try and peel back stick onto me... Nice sharp elbow is coming your way."

Andy Carroll: "You will just about reach my knees you midget!"

The Hammers duo banter on Twitter

"U know what, f*ck the lot of you, u will never get another tweet from me again, you just don't get it do you. Bye bye."

Danny Gabbidon tweets an angry message aimed at the fans after West Ham's home defeat by Aston Villa

"I'm so exciting that every time I play, the fans want to have sex with me."

Paolo Di Canio

"It was frustrating to join after a World Cup and have the manager ask what position I played but I continued to push forward for six months."

Argentina's Javier Mascherano is left unimpressed by Alan Pardew who preferred the likes of Hayden Mullins over him

"I should be captaining Argentina! What went wrong?"

Hayden Mullins on keeping Javier Mascherano out of the Hammers side

"Playing for England won't faze Carlton [Cole] at all. One of his great attributes is that he doesn't think too much, so I think he'll be OK."

Robert Green

"I want the West Ham fans to know that we're going to win something before I finish my career here. Otherwise I will kill myself."

Paolo Di Canio taking extreme measures

"I am ashamed. I am shocked at the way we played. We played like a bunch of drunks."

Yossi Benayoun after West Ham's 6-0 defeat to Reading

"When I kiss the West Ham badge people say, 'It's because he wants a new contract'. If I wanted a new contract I'd come in here and lick the club's arse."

Paolo Di Canio before signing for Charlton

"My wife told me, 'When you are running on the pitch, you are not like you are in Bordeaux, so you have to do something'. She booked me a week at Merano where we went and I did some fitness work."

Julien Faubert gets footballing advice from wife Pamela

"How could anyone think the side would be better off without me?"

Paolo Di Canio after being axed from the team by Glenn Roeder

"I watched 'The Simpsons Movie' the other day and I saw Homer do it, and I thought it looked hilarious, so [I thought] I'll do it if I score."

Michail Antonio explains his spinning-floor goal celebration in a win over Sunderland

"This is the perfect solution for me here. I love to have sex at Upton Park. Not real sex, you understand... You know what I mean."

Paolo Di Canio

"I'm not stupid. I'm not afraid to change countries. It'll still be better than here. At West Ham, I've wasted my time."

Alou Diarra blasts the club

"It's disappointing to be dropped from any team – even my mates' fantasy league team!"

Robert Green sees the funny side after being omitted from the England squad

Q: "What would you get Carl Jenkinson for Christmas?"

A: "Some banter if I could, because he has absolutely zero. He is the weirdest man ever."

Andy Carroll on Carl Jenkinson

"It's handy to look up and see we have that big lump up front."

Jack Collison on Andy Carroll

"I said 'f*ck off'. He said, 'No Paolo, this is Alex'. I said, 'Alex who? Is this you, you mother-f*cker?'"

Paolo Di Canio on his response to Sir Alex Ferguson who rang to try and sign him

"I understand nothing when Rio [Ferdinand] and Frank [Lampard] are talking. They speak Cocknik."

Eyal Berkovic

"The players have got plenty of food in the dressing room so he couldn't have been hungry!"

Robert Green after Spurs striker Jermain Defoe allegedly bit Javier Mascherano

"I like to think Lee Bowyer will be a player to watch out for next season."

Lee Bowyer on Lee Bowyer

"When I see all my legs out, I have confidence. I look at my muscles and they look big and feel strong. With big shorts, I can't see my muscles at all."

Paolo Di Canio

"Feel stupid for the tweets I made when I was 16, the big man's going to kill me!! Sorry @AndyTCarroll"

New Hammer Diego Poyet apologises for a mean tweet he posted three years earlier mocking then-Liverpool striker Andy Carroll

"A big thanks to @diegopoyet7 for agreeing to make my morning cuppa every morning for the next month!!"

Andy Carroll takes the apology in good spirits

"The specialist did these tests, pulled the leg every way imaginable and took some x-rays. After lengthy analysis he told me, 'Your knee is f*cked'."

Julian Dicks

"When I scored that goal to knock out Manchester United, it was like having sex with Madonna."

Paolo Di Canio on his goal for West Ham against Man United in the 2001 FA Cup

"I'm 28 now and they say you peak at 28 – so my best years are still ahead of me."

Kieron Dyer

THE FUNNIEST WEST HAM QUOTES... EVER!

SAY THAT AGAIN?

"There are two kinds of people. When there is a fire, some people come with oil to make the fire bigger and some come with the water. I come with water."

Avram Grant the fireman

"I have been surprised so many times this year – so I am not surprised that I am surprised."

Gianfranco Zola on talk of a bid for West Brom's Graham Dorrans

"Being given chances, and not taking them. That's what life is all about."

Ron Greenwood

Say That Again?

"If the heat is too hot in the kitchen you get out, but I am prepared to stand there and be counted."

Glenn Roeder likes a cliche

"It's so vital if you can win the game 1-0 rather than lose it 1-0."

Billy Bonds

"I won't be losing any sleepless nights over it."

Alan Pardew

"I can see the carrot at the end of the tunnel."

Stuart Pearce

"One minute you can be riding the crest of a wave and the next minute you can be down. It's a funny old game. It's a great leveller, and you can't get too cock-a-hoop about things. It's an old cliche but you've got to take each game as it comes and keep working at it. In playing or management, you're only as good as your last game."

Billy Bonds really loves a cliche

"In terms of the Richter scale this defeat was a force eight gale."

John Lyall

Say That Again?

"For us to overtake them has been a massive undertaking."

Sam Allardyce

"Playing with wingers is more effective against European sides like Brazil, than English sides like Wales."

Ron Greenwood is not great at geography

"We're clearly a top-six side, even though the league doesn't lie."

Harry Redknapp on West Ham stuck at the bottom of the table after six matches

"If you take liberties with the opposition, they'll pull your trousers down."

Billy Bonds

"What fascinates me – and this is probably where Mussolini and I are very different – is the way he was able to go against his morals to achieve his goals."

Paolo Di Canio on the fascist leader

"Unfortunately, we don't get a second chance. We've already played them twice."

Trevor Brooking

Say That Again?

"I could use a cliche, but that's not me. The one thing you can't do is worry about tomorrow."

Glenn Roeder

"Nothing surprises me any more in the Premiership, but that surprises me."

Alan Curbishley on the delay in signing Kieron Dyer

"We've got a couple of milestones around our neck."

Alan Pardew is lucky they aren't millstones

FROM THE TERRACE

"His name is Rio and he watches from the stand."

Chant about former defender Rio Ferdinand, to the tune of Duran Duran's 'Rio', after he was banned for missing a drugs test in 2003

"He's got a bird's nest on his head."

Sung to Everton's Marouane Fellaini

Southampton fans: "We are Southampton, we're going to Brazil."

West Ham fans: "We are West Ham United, we won the World Cup."

"He's coming for you, he's coming for you,

Harry Potter, he's coming for you."

Bald midfielder Jonjo Shelvey on his

uncanny resemblance to Lord Voldemort

"We've got Di Canio, you've got our stereos."

Hammers supporters away at Liverpool

"One shot, we only had one shot!"

West Ham fans to Arsenal after sneaking a

1-0 victory

"You're nothing special, we lose every week."

Manchester City thrash Hammers 6-0

"We've got Payet, Dimitri Payet! I just don't think you understand. He's Super Slav's man, he's better than Zidane. We've got Dimitri Payet!"

West Ham fans when Dimitri Payet was the flavour of the month

"F*ck off Payet, Dimitri Payet, we just don't want you anymore. You've got some f*cking front, you money-grabbing c*nt, f*ck off Dimitri Payet!"

An X-rated song to the now-despised Dimitri Payet after stating his desire to go on strike

"If you made a lot of money selling biscuits, buy our club."

Fans sing to the tune of the Club biscuit commercial in tribute to biscuit baron Eggert Magnusson

"We can see you. We can see you. We can see you holding hands!"

At Brighton, referring to the town's standing as the gay capital of England

"Oh when the Saints go 3-1 down."

West Ham fans remind their Southampton counterparts of the scoreline – to the tune of their own traditional chant

"Wenger in! Wenger out! In out, in out, shake it all about! Do the Arsene Wenger and you turn around. That's what it's all about! Whoa, Arsene Wenger!"

West Ham fans poke fun at Arsenal, with this chant based on the famous 'Hokey Cokey' song

"Who's the midget in the suit?"

Vertically-challenged Bolton manager Sammy Lee gets a chant from the fans

"Does your butler know you're here?"

West Ham supporters to the posh Fulham ones at Craven Cottage

"Vera's dead, Vera's dead, Vera's dead!"

Hammers fans away at Man City after the death of Coronation Street character Vera Duckworth

"Lasagne, whoao! Lasagne, whoao! We laughed ourselves to bits, when Tottenham got the sh*ts!"

West Ham fans to Tottenham after they suffered food poisoning before the final game of the season, costing them a Champions League spot

"There's only one Prince Philip!"

Hammers at Mohammed Al Fayed's Fulham

"Stick the rugby, stick the rugby, stick the rugby up your arse."

Hammers supporters away at Wigan

"We're West Ham United, we play on the floor."

Fans upset about the direct style of play under Sam Allardyce. The manager responded by saying, "I'm sick of all that rubbish"

"How sh*t must you be – it's only 1-0!"

The away faithful at Nottingham Forest, who then went and scored another four

"When you're sat in row Z, and the ball hits your head, that's Zamora!"

Supporters on the striker Bobby Zamora

"That's why you're going down."

Hammers respond to theTottenham chant of: "You are our feeder club"

"We've got a Chicharito, so much better than Defoe and Iheanacho, Slaven's Chicharito. Our little Mexican pace man, down at West Ham. Javier Javier, oh Javier Javier. He bangs them in (x3), Chicharito (x4)."

Javier Hernandez chant sung to the tune of Ritchie Valens' La Bamba

"Everyone had a rattle and they went just to enjoy the game. If that sounds a rose-tinted or nostalgic memory, I'm sorry, but it's true. Then, for me, and my dad, it was a cheese roll at a little cafe up the road, the 106 bus and then the 227 back to Polar."

The final word goes to Harry Redknapp –
on watching West Ham as a supporter

Printed in Poland
by Amazon Fulfillment
Poland Sp. z o.o., Wrocław